S0-BOR-158

333.95   Banks, Martin
BAN
           Endangered wildlife

$19.93

DATE			

GLENEAGLES COMMUNITY
SCHOOL LIBRARY.

BAKER & TAYLOR BOOKS

ENDANGERED WILDLIFE

Martin Banks

GLENEAGLES COMMUNITY
SCHOOL LIBRARY.

ROURKE ENTERPRISES INC.
Vero Beach, Florida 32964

World Issues

Endangered Wildlife
Food or Famine?
International Terrorism
Nuclear Weapons
Population Growth
The Arms Trade
The Energy Crisis
The Environment
The International Drug Trade
World Health

Cover: A tiger at a water hole
Frontispiece: A young orangutan in the wild

Text © 1988 Rourke Enterprises Inc.
PO Box 3328, Vero Beach, Florida 32964

All rights reserved. No part of this book may be reproduced or utilized in any form or by any means electronic or mechanical including photocopying, recording or by any information storage and retrieval system without permission in writing from the publishers.

Printed in Italy.

Picture Acknowledgments
Biofotos 32 (Heather Angel), 39 (Brian Rogers); Bruce Coleman 11 (Melinda Berge), 15 (WWF/ Paul Barruel), 19 (Peter Jackson), 24 (Alain Compost), 25 (WWF/Timm Rautert), 28 (WWF/H. Jungius), 29 (Norman Tomalin), 30 (L. C. Marigo), 33 (Francisco Erize), 37 (B. & C. Calhoun); Tim Fargher 14 (by kind permission of Tim Walker); Eric and David Hosking 31, 42; Frank Lane cover (Leonard Lee Rue), frontispiece (Dani-Jeske), 8 (Dani-Jeske), 16 (M. J. Thomas), 20 (S. McCutcheon); Tony Morrison 22; Oxford Scientific Films 12 (G. I. Bernard), 17 (Michael Fogden), 26 (Tony Martin), 34 (Stephen Mills), 38 (Alastair Shay), 40 (M. A. Chappell), 43 (Nick Woods); Oxford University Museum 13; Sheridan Photo Library 10, 23; Survival Anglia 18 (Liz & Tony Bomford), 35 (Dieter & Mary Plage), 36 (Cindy Buxton, Annie Price); ZEFA 21.

Library of Congress Cataloging-in-Publication Data
Banks, Martin, 1947-
  Endangered wildlife / Martin Banks.
    p. cm. (World issues)
  Bibliography: p.
  Includes index.
  Summary: Explains the difference between endangered and threatened animal species, why animals become extinct, and efforts to protect wildlife.
  ISBN 0-86592-284-5
  1. Wildlife conservation—Juvenile literature.   2. Endangered species—Juvenile literature.   [1. Wildlife conservation.   2. Rare animals.   3. Extinction (Biology)]   I. Title.   II. Series: World issues (Vero Beach, Fla.)
QL83.B36   1988
333.95'416—dc19   88-5970
                                                   CIP
                                                   AC

Contents

1. Introduction   8

2. The causes of extinction   9

3. The world's wildlife today   16

4. Conservation in action   23

5. Redressing the balance   32

6. The future   38

Glossary   44

Index   45

1 Introduction

"No provisions are given to the wild crane, but the heavens and earth are his."

Buddhist Poet

When a species of animal or plant becomes extinct, it ceases to exist on earth. This may seem a very obvious statement, but it is important to remember exactly what "endangered" means, and what a "threatened" species is in danger of becoming. Should it be important to us if an animal becomes extinct? Should we be concerned that so many species are currently treading the same path?

Extinction is not merely a sad or bad thing. There are many reasons why we should try to halt the continuing decline in the number and variety of animal and plant species with which we share the earth. Humans, animals and their environment have a rich and complex, interdependent relationship – that which affects one part of this network affects the whole. There are financial factors too; for example, wild animals can be successfully raised under careful management and then culled, without detriment to their populations, to provide food for people. Then there are moral and aesthetic considerations. Wild animals have an equal right to share this planet with us. What right have we to kill them and to spoil the wild places in which they live? We should consider future generations of people too. Is it not better to hand down to them a world that is still inhabited by as diverse and as fine an array of species as possible?

Human beings are the most powerful creatures on earth. We possess the ability to influence the balance of nature around us, for better or for worse. So far, at least in our recent history, this influence has sadly been for the worse. In the last few centuries, the human population has increased enormously, while animal species have become extinct at a directly proportional rate. Still more species are likely to become extinct in the near future. But, with enlightened thinking and rapid action on our part, it may be possible to stem this tide even in the face of our own soaring population.

We can never bring back those species that are already extinct, but we can try to prevent an already tragically long list from growing any longer.

The orangutan is one of many species whose existence is endangered by human activities. By what right are we doing this?

2 The causes of extinction

"The white man treats his mother, the earth, and his brother, the sky, as things to be bought, plundered, sold like sheep or bright beads."
Chief Seattle of the Duwamish League, 1854

During the millions of years in which life has existed on earth, it has been host to an enormous variety of animal species, many of which have died out naturally during the course of evolution. For example, the great reptiles of prehistoric times, such as the dinosaurs, eventually became extinct because they could not adapt to climatic and vegetation changes. Much later, mammals such as the woolly mammoth and the saber-toothed tiger,

Extinction can be a natural phenomenon; dinosaurs like this spinosaurus vanished millions of years before humans appeared on earth.

9

followed them into oblivion. No animal species is guaranteed a life of more than a few million years before it evolves into new forms or dies out completely. This process of natural extinction continues today. However, in modern times the rate at which species have been becoming extinct has increased dramatically. In the last three centuries, well over a hundred species of mammals and birds have disappeared, mainly as a direct result of human influence. At the same time, many other species have been so drastically reduced in numbers that they too are in great danger of becoming extinct within the next few years.

Humankind exerts its influence on wild animals in a number of ways. We hunt for food, skins and hides; we even kill animals for sport, while certain species are deliberately attacked because they are regarded as pests or nuisances, or perhaps are feared in some way. Overhunting is one of the main causes of recent

We have human records of the more recently extinct species. This cave painting from France shows a woolly mammoth.

species extinction. In North America, two species, the buffalo and the passenger pigeon, once existed in vast numbers. But the coming of white settlers put an end to this. The buffalo was very nearly wiped out, and the passenger pigeon was completely wiped out.

In the case of the buffalo, this species had long been hunted by the American Indians, who depended on it for many of their day-to-day needs, particularly the supply of meat and hides. Yet the Indians, with their simple hunting methods, never had any chance of making serious inroads on the buffalo population. That was left to white settlers. In the space of two hundred years (1700–1900), the millions of buffalo that once existed on the prairies of North America had been reduced to just a few dozen animals. The reason? Overhunting by white men. Equipped with firearms, they initially hunted buffalo for their meat, but later they killed them simply for sport and because the animals were so easy to kill. Fortunately, in the buffalo case, it was realized just in time that it required complete protection and, today, its numbers have again increased to the stage where some sizable herds, numbering several thousand animals, can be seen in special reserves.

The passenger pigeon was not so fortunate. At one time, it was probably more numerous than any other species of bird. Single flocks were estimated to contain over two billion birds and, as they flew over, they sometimes darkened the sky. Yet, today, not a single passenger pigeon remains. The last recorded survivor died in a zoo in 1914, several years after the last small flocks of wild birds had disappeared. It would seem that the enormous flocks were overhunted, their

numbers ultimately reduced to the point where the birds could no longer breed successfully until, slowly, the remaining population dwindled to nil.

Humans have other, less direct methods of hastening the extinction of a species. These include introducing alien species

Buffalo in Custer National Park. Before the arrival of white men, herds of buffalo thousands strong roamed these plains.

that disrupt the delicate balance of the existing fauna and flora. Although wild species have been introduced into a number of different countries with varying results, the worst culprits tend to be domestic animals – either predators, such as dogs, cats and pigs, which kill and eat animals and their eggs, or herbivores, such as goats, donkeys, cattle and rabbits, which may compete with native wild species for food and at the same time spoil the natural habitat by overgrazing. There are many examples of species that have been exterminated by this means, particularly on islands and island chains, where the total populations of animal species are limited anyway. Faced with predators against which they have no natural defenses, or planteaters that destroy their habitat, the original inhabitants soon die out. Often humankind, whose actions were responsible for upsetting the natural balance in the first place, has been quite oblivious of what has taken place.

Losses due to introduced animals have been especially heavy in places like New Zealand, the Hawaiian Islands, the Galapagos Islands and the Mascarenes, including Mauritius in the Indian Ocean. In these places, many of the original animal species have been lost.

Rabbits, introduced to New Zealand by white settlers, have caused great damage to the indigenous wildlife.

It was on Mauritius that a flightless bird called the dodo used to exist. It was a creature of improbable appearance. Plump and turkey-sized, it had enormous feet, a huge beak and tiny wings that were useless for flight. The neighboring islands of Reunion and Rodriguez each boasted their own flightless species,

A dodo, painted by John Savery, around 1650. The dodo is the best known of all extinct species, perhaps because of its extraordinary appearance.

called solitaires. It the mid-1600s, Dutch and Portuguese settlers colonized the islands, bringing with them dogs, cats,

13

The elegant blaawbok, or bluebuck, was one of many victims of the white man's gun in Africa.

pigs and even monkeys. These ate either the hapless birds or their eggs. The settlers themselves found the birds easy to catch though not very good to eat. To have evolved in such an extraordinary fashion, these birds must have been isolated on the islands for thousands of years. Yet all three species were extinct before 1800. All we have to commemorate the dodo, which was extinct by about 1680 (within a few decades of the colonization of Mauritius), are a few sketches and descriptions handed down from eye witnesses, a few bones in a museum, and a well-known saying . . .

The dodo and passenger pigeon are perhaps the two best-known examples of extinct birds. Another is the great auk, the

last pair of which were killed at Eldey Rock, Iceland, in 1844. Many mammals, too, have been wiped out. The quagga, a species of zebra, and the blaawbok, an antelope, were both decimated by white settlers in South Africa as a result of exhaustive overhunting at a time when no thought was given to the future of any wild animal species. The blaawbok was already extinct by 1800, five museum specimens being the only record we have of its existence. The quagga lasted until 1883, when the last survivor died in a zoo.

Extinct before 1900	
Mammals	*Birds*
Quagga	Great Auk
Blaawbok	Dodo
Patagonian giant	Moa
Ground sloth	Aukland Island rail
Steller's sea cow	Mysterious starling
Atlas bear	White swamp hen
Cape lion	Spectacled
Sea mink	cormorant
Gilbert's rat	Labrador duck
kangaroo	Mamo
Antarctic wolf	Akialea
Hairy-eared	Seychelles green
mouse	parakeet
Jamaican rice rat	Fernbird

Extinct after 1900	
Mammals	*Birds*
Barbary lion	Passenger pigeon
Bubal hartebeest	Carolina parakeet
Rufous gazelle	Heath hen
Long-eared kit fox	Crested shelduck
White-tailed rat	Pink-headed duck
Thylacine	Huia
Christmas Island	Auckland Island
shrew	merganser
Cuban solenodon	Delande's coucal

For some species, there is no tangible record of their existence at all. Steller's sea cow was a huge aquatic mammal that once lived in the Bering Sea, the cold waters between North America and Russia. Discovered in 1791, it was hunted into extinction within thirty years.

Since 1900, few mammal and bird species have been exterminated, but some have been lost to us forever during this period. The huia, a black, crow-sized bird that inhabited the forests of New Zealand, was remarkable in that the male and female each had a differently shaped bill. The male had a short, straight bill, which he used to tap trees in order to disturb insects. The female had a longer, curved bill, which she used to collect them. The two members of a pair depended on each other to find food. Yet this unique method of feeding cannot now be observed, since huias are believed to have become extinct as a result of the loss of forest land in New Zealand.

Today, we are beginning to realize that the extinction of a species is the ultimate failure. In the last few decades very few animals are known, or believed, to have become extinct (for extinction is not always easy to prove). Yet it seems inevitable that more species will reach the point where their numbers become so low that, even with scientific and financial help to protect the last few survivors, all efforts will prove insufficient to prevent their extinction. For example, there is the Tasmanian wolf (or thylacine), a strange marsupial predator that may still exist in its Tasmanian home, but has not been reliably observed for over fifty years. And the North American dusky seaside sparrow will probably be extinct by the time you read this book. Its last surviving members are incapable of replenishing their numbers since they are all males.

A dusky seaside sparrow. Does it matter if this insignificant-looking bird dies out?

3
The world's wildlife today

"Yesterday a jungle, tomorrow a town."
Advertisement slogan for the United Motor Works

Today there is a growing awareness of the plight faced by so many forms of wildlife. "Endangered species" and "threatened wildlife" have become bywords, at least to those of us living in the Developed World. In recent years, we have come to know a great deal more about the environment in which we live and the animal species with which we share it. Nowadays, it is almost unheard of for a population of animals to become extinct without strenuous efforts being made to preserve the last surviving members of the species.

While this is certainly an improvement, it still does not give us cause for complacency. The great majority of threatened

Constructing a drainage channel through wetland habitat in Wales. Wetlands are threatened all around the world as pressure for agricultural land grows.

species live in areas of the world where a multitude of factors continue to work against them. Paramount among these is the continuing destruction of the natural habitats where animals live. The ways in which this happens are many and varied – the felling of forests for lumber and to clear the land for agriculture; the drainage and irrigation projects that are carried out to convert marshy areas to farmland; the damming of rivers; mineral and mining developments; the cultivation of land; and the encroachment of towns and cities, roads and railroads. All of these things, so necessary to our concept of progress, are detrimental to wildlife.

Rain forest in Costa Rica. Only a fraction of the species contained in the world's great forests have been identified.

In the last few years much attention has been focused on the plight of one of the most diverse habitats of all, the tropical rain forests. It is a staggering thought that, in some areas, rain forests are being cut down at the rate of about 96 acres per minute. If their destruction continues at this rate, then 1 percent of the remaining forests, together with the wildlife they contain, will be lost each year. Apart from the problems caused by the consequent soil erosion and local climatic changes, the loss

17

of the world's rain forests spells disaster for many notable animal species. Predominant among them are primates, such as the gorillas and chimpanzees of Africa, many species of monkeys and marmosets in South America, and the orangutan and the gibbon in Southeast Asia. In Madagascar, the forests have already largely disappeared, leaving a unique selection of primitive primates, called lemurs, struggling to survive in the remaining isolated pockets of forest.

In most tropical countries, the major part of the human population is still rurally based and therefore reliant on agriculture and the land for its survival. To these people, wildlife conservation means little, if anything at all. Wild animals are more likely to represent either an important source of food or a way of earning income.

They may even present a potential threat, where the needs of animals and people conflict. So, while we in the West may view the conservation of wildlife and of

An area of rain forest 25 square miles in size is estimated to contain the following; up to 1,500 species of flowering plants, 750 species of trees, 400 bird species, 100 different reptiles, 60 amphibians. Of the invertebrates, like butterflies and many other insects (which are far too numerous to count accurately), there may be as many as 4,000 species.

A black lemur carrying its young. Their survival in the wild depends on the fate of the Madagascar forests.

natural resources in the Developing World as important issues, the values and attitudes of the indigenous population are quite likely, through necessity, to be very different. For example, we often hear of the continued poaching of Africa's elephants for their valuable ivory, or of the rhinos of Africa and Asia for their horns (which in many areas are still believed to have magical and medicinal powers) and of the continued hunting and killing of threatened species of primates in the rain forests of South America. When we hear of such things, it is worth remembering that the local people may still depend on these activities at least in part for income, even for survival.

Poaching of elephants will continue as long as tourists are prepared to pay a high price for ivory statues like these.

The extreme north and south of the globe, the Arctic and Antarctic regions, might be thought of as still relatively safe for animals. By and large, they present an inhospitable climate for humans to live in and their geographic location makes them difficult to reach and therefore harder to interfere with. Unfortunately, this is no longer completely true. In the far north of Canada, in Alaska and in Siberia, the exploration and development of mineral resources are altering the environment. Modern means of transportation, such as aircraft, ships and

19

snowmobiles, make traveling within the polar regions far less arduous than it used to be. As more people move into these areas, so the pressures on wildlife increase, not only from direct hunting (since there are more efficient weapons available too), but also from the consequent pollution of these fragile habitats.

Much the same can be said about the seas and oceans, which cover three-quarters of the earth's surface and which play a vital part in supporting life systems and in governing climate. They are constantly under threat from human activities. Although the ocean is one of the most important sources of food left to a growing world population, a combination of pollution,

Searching for gold in Alaska, where mining creates serious pollution problems.

mining, and dumping of toxic and even nuclear wastes, all combine to threaten both the oceans and the immense wealth of wildlife they support. At the same time, overfishing threatens to substantially alter the ecological balance of the seas, while continued overhunting by certain nations threatens the greatest of all sea mammals, the whales, and is putting the future of some species in immediate jeopardy.

Despite the fact that modern ideas of wildlife conservation stemmed from the countries of the Developed World, they have not always set a particularly good example for others to follow. Although North America now has an excellent system of national parks and reserves in which wildlife is conserved, there is relatively little room left for wildlife outside these areas. In Europe too, species like the European bison and the beaver were almost totally wiped out before their plight was recognized. Today, the larger species that were once numerous throughout Europe are largely confined to the relatively small areas of parks and reserves

This stretch of Indian Ocean shoreline in South Africa is heavily polluted with industrial wastes.

Quinine bark from the Amazon provides the main ingredient for antimalarial drugs. The native people knew of its properties long before it was "discovered" by science.

that have been set aside for their protection. For some predatory animals, like wolves and bears, the balance of nature has been so upset that either insufficient habitats or inadequate supplies of their natural prey now exist to allow them to survive in anything but tiny fragmented groups.

All around the world, wildlife and wild places are shrinking in the face of human-kind's relentless expansion. There are valid reasons why it is essential that we stop this process, at least in its most harmful forms, before it is too late. Many animal and plant species are of economic value to us. For example, many plant species contain the active ingredients of important drugs that we use to combat a whole range of illnesses. Some animal or plant species can be crossbred to provide increased vigor and greater resistance to disease. It is worth remembering that, despite our technological expertise and our great advances in the fields of science, we are still unable to recreate any living thing once it has ceased to exist.

4 Conservation in action

"Conservation is like freedom. It can only be maintained by constant vigilance."

H.R.H. Prince Philip, Duke of Edinburgh; Address to the Australian Conservation Foundation

Wildlife conservation is by no means a recent concept. The idea of preserving stocks of animals to allow them to breed for our ultimate benefit has been put into practice at various times throughout history. The Norman kings of England set aside areas of forestland to preserve deer and other animals for hunting. These parks, or chases, as they were called, were rigidly protected and severe punishments were meted out to anyone found poaching the animals they contained. The Persian kings called their hunting parks "paradises." And in Africa, long before the present system of national parks came into being, a Zulu king established a game park to preserve stocks of elephants and other large game animals.

Killing animals for sport has been popular throughout history. The design on this plate shows a Persian king hunting deer in the sixth century.

Since the beginning of this century, however, a number of organizations have been established that are specifically dedicated to the conservation of endangered wildlife. The International Union for Conservation of Nature and Natural Resources (IUCN), founded in 1948, is an independent body whose principal objectives are to monitor the state of the world's living resources and to decide the scientific priorities of conservation. From its headquarters in Switzerland, the IUCN coordinates the work of a large body of scientists who work through six commissions. Each of these is involved with a particular aspect of conservation. Another organization, the International Council for Bird Preservation (ICBP), was founded in 1922. Together, the two organizations have produced what might be termed the conservationist's bible in a set of books that contain all the available information on the plant and animal species that are known to be "in danger." Each listed species is graded on a scale of rarity, according to what is known about its current status and all the factors that threaten its future existence. The *Red Data*

IUCN status coding for *Red Data Book* species is as follows:
Extinct: Not definitely located in the wild in the past 50 years.
Endangered: In danger of extinction, future survival unlikely if current factors working against it continue unchanged.
Vulnerable: Likely to become endangered in near future if situation remains unchanged.
Rare: Species having small world populations, not presently either endangered or vulnerable, but possibly at risk.

Books, as they are known, are the result of painstaking research, both in the field and in compiling and updating the data they contain. The IUCN has recently established a conservation monitoring center in Cambridge, England, where this work is now carried out.

Much of the funding for conservation projects undertaken around the world by the IUCN is provided by the World Wildlife Fund (WWF). Created in 1961, it is probably the best-known conservation body in the world. There can be few people who aren't familiar with its symbol, the giant panda, or its basic aims, to raise money and further the cause of wildlife protection. Since its formation as a fund-raising charity, the WWF has raised huge sums of money to support more than 7,000

The Javan rhinoceros is close to the top of the IUCN's list of endangered mammals.

projects in 135 different countries, many of them carried out by the IUCN. The money is spent in a variety of ways, such as purchasing land for reserves, paying staff and providing funds for equipment, fencing, scientific studies and surveys.

One of the better-known undertakings with which the WWF has been associated is "Project Tiger," an effort to save the magnificent wild cats in India. Project Tiger is an example of how a well-organized project inspired by a particular species can benefit many other species too. By the early 1970s, it was estimated that only 2,000 tigers remained in the whole of India, their last stronghold. Their numbers had fallen drastically due to continued hunting and the loss of their jungle home through deforestation and land cultivation. With backing from the WWF, the Indian government began to create and enlarge a series of wildlife reserves, not only for the protection of tigers, but also with the aim of conserving all the other animal species in these areas. No longer threatened by poaching and hunting, the stocks of deer and other species that the tigers prey on began to increase and, consequently, so did the number of tigers. So protection for the tiger, which stands at the top of its food chain, has had the benefit of protecting many other plant and animal species too. New reserves have been added to the original list, and the future for the tiger, and indeed many of India's other endangered species, now looks considerably brighter.

Ironically, the WWF's symbol, the giant

A rare picture of a giant panda in the wild, where they are notoriously difficult to observe.

panda, is facing a crisis of a different sort in its only home, the bamboo forests of China. Less than one thousand of these spectacular animals, which are related to racoons, are believed to exist in the wild. Despite a great deal of research, relatively little is known about their habits and biology. Their staple diet is bamboo and, in several reserves where the pandas still live, the bamboo has been flowering, after which it dies off. WWF and Chinese scientists are currently trying to determine how to safeguard the survival of this fascinating species.

Some countries refuse to stop whaling though the industry makes an insignificant contribution to their economies.

Some organizations exist to promote the conservation of an individual group or species of animal at international level. The plight of the whale, which has suffered greatly from overhunting by a number of countries, has been much publicized. An International Whaling Commission (IWC) was set up with the purpose of

A Greenpeace boat trying to disrupt a whale hunt. Direct action like this has done much to publicize the plight of the whales.

controlling the hunting of these creatures so that their stocks could be built up. It has not been completely successful in this task. Since it was founded, the IWC has sought to restrict hunting by establishing strict quotas on the numbers of whales that are caught annually by whalers. These quotas vary according to the comparative rarity of each species of whale. While many countries have cooperated, some continue to ignore these regulations. More recently, the IWC has tried to impose a moratorium, or total ban, on the hunting of certain species of whale. They have been hindered by the refusal of just a few nations, such as Iceland, Japan and Norway, either to reduce their levels of hunting or to stop commerical whaling altogether, even in the face of increasing public criticism from around the world.

The FFPS (Fauna and Flora Preservation Society) is one of the oldest conservation societies in the world. One of its best-known achievements was the part it played in saving the white oryx of the Arabian desert from the brink of extinction. The Arabian oryx, which is also the society's motif, fell victim to motorized hunting parties, which practically exterminated the species in the wild by the early 1970s. But, acting with commendable foresight some ten years earlier, the FFPS had organized the capture of three of the last surviving members of the species and transported them to the Phoenix Zoo in Arizona, for safe-keeping. There, with the addition of a few more animals from other collections, a sizable herd was built up and later divided among several zoos across the United States to lessen the chance of disease wiping out this captive population. By 1980, well over 150 oryx existed in captivity, yet none had been seen in the wild for several years. Now, small groups are once again to be seen in the deserts of their homeland, thanks to an apparently successful reintroduction program. Part of the success of this program has been due to the involvement of local tribesmen, who act as guardians to

An Arabian oryx in the Jordanian desert. This is one of the most notable successes of captive breeding programs.

the newly released animals.

Even more recently, another critically endangered species has become the focus of a major appeal by the FFPS. In 1979, considerable publicity was given to the plight of the mountain gorillas of Central Africa. At that time, there were probably less than 350 left in their main home, the Virunga volcanoes, which straddle the borders of three countries – Rwanda, Zaire and Uganda. This was largely the result of poaching, coupled with the destruction of their forest home. Prompt action was essential if the animals were to survive. A "Mountain Gorilla Project" was set up with considerable publicity and many fund-raising events. The project is designed to increase the protection of the remaining forests in the Virungas, to shield the gorillas themselves from the effects of poaching, and to provide an education program aimed at making the local people more aware of the value of both the forests that still survive and the gorillas that live in them. One aspect of the Mountain Gorilla Project has proved particularly interesting. Owing to the increased publicity, visits by both Africans and foreign tourists to see the gorillas have greatly increased. The park staff have been able to accustom some of the gorilla groups to visits by such tourist parties. This tourist trade is beginning to represent an important source of income for Rwanda, the country that has actively led the way in trying to improve the situation. Tourism is therefore providing another incentive for conserving the gorillas. However, the survival of the mountain gorilla into the next century still depends predominantly on whether the indigenous peoples of its native countries come to understand the value of preserving the surviving forests.

The decimation of wildlife by hunting, habitat destruction and upsetting the balance of nature has been happening for many years. But, quite recently, a new threat has arisen – the trade of certain wild animal species and their products. Many species are in demand for their skins or furs, which are used to make expensive adornments for the rich. Fashions change from time to time, but the animals that have suffered the most are spotted cats (such as the leopard and cheetah) and crocodiles and snakes, whose skins are used to make handbags and shoes.

Fur coats on sale. The fur trade claims the lives of millions of animals each year.

Other species are also commercially valuable for certain parts of their bodies – musk from the Himalayan musk deer, horn from the rhinoceros and, of course, ivory from elephant tusks. At the same time, the trade in live animals has increased, due to demand in many Western countries for rate pets. Particularly at risk are all species of primates, especially the smaller monkeys and marmosets; colorful birds, such as parrots; large and small reptiles, especially crocodilians, snakes, lizards and tortoises; many species of tropical butterflies; and even snails and spiders. In 1973, the Convention on International Trade in Endangered Species of Wild Fauna and Flora (CITES) came into force, after ten

This woolly monkey, one of the world's most endangered mammals, is on sale as a pet in Brazil.

The demand for exotic pets has endangered even the red-kneed, bird-eating spider from Mexico.

countries had agreed to ban all trade in the animal species then listed as endangered. Today, nearly a hundred countries have ratified the CITES agreement, but the illegal trade continues while many countries have still not joined this voluntary ban. Some species, like the red-kneed tarantula spider of Mexico, which is in increasing demand as a household pet in the U.S. and Europe, may not be able to withstand the continual drain on their populations for much longer. The IUCN Wildlife Trade Monitoring Unit maintains an increasing number of voluntary offices around the world, with the specific purpose of studying and halting, wherever possible, the movement and commercial sale of wild animal species.

Endangered Mammals	*Endangered Birds*	*Endangered Reptiles*
Mountain gorilla	Californian condor	Nile crocodile
Blue whale	Mauritius kestrel	Leatherback turtle
Asiatic lion	Philippines eagle	Radiated tortoise
Mediterranean monk seal	St. Vincent parrot	Galapagos giant tortoise
Javan rhinoceros	Japanese crested ibis	Olive Ridley turtle
Somali wild ass	Siberian crane	Spectacled caiman
Pigmy hog	Noisy scrub bird	Gharial
Woolly spider monkey	Chatham Island robin	

5 Redressing the balance

"Living species today, let us remember, are the end products of twenty million centuries of evolution; absolutely nothing can be done when the species has finally gone, when the last pair has died out."

Sir Peter Scott: Conference on captive breeding of endangered species

The influence of conservation organizations has been increasingly effective in bringing protection for animal species in the wild. However, some species have reached such critically low numbers, mainly as a result of humankind's impact on them, that active intervention on our part may prove the only hope of saving them. The Arabian oryx is a case in point, a species that actually became extinct in the wild for over a decade, but which, through planned and careful management, survived and multiplied in captivity to the stage where a reintroduction program has become possible.

In the past, zoos have frequently been criticized as consumers and exploiters of wildlife. Yet today, with our increasing understanding of the needs of animals, more and more species are being successfully maintained and bred in captivity. This has a twofold benefit. First, it

Perhaps the main function of a good zoo is to increase people's interest in wildlife and its conservation.

reduces the demand for animals from the wild, many of which are now less readily obtainable thanks to stricter controls on the animal trade. Second, it means that members of threatened species that are held in captivity are becoming increasingly available for reintroduction projects. For, in the worst cases, this may be the only means left to us to reestablish a species in the wild.

There are a number of well-known species that owe their current existence to captive breeding. The European bison is today found in several reserves in Eastern Europe, notably in Poland and the U.S.S.R. But this has occurred only because

Pere David's deer were saved from extinction by captive breeding.

small numbers were carefully preserved under semi-captive conditions earlier this century, when overhunting had virtually exterminated them in the wild. Przewalski's wild horse, the only surviving ancestor of our domestic horse, has not been seen for a number of years in its native home in the vast open steppes of Mongolia, yet several hundred animals live in various zoos around the world. Plans are afoot to try to reintroduce some of them into a suitable area in the Gobi desert in the near future. Pere David's deer (named after the French missionary who discovered it) is a native of China, but it has been extinct there since 1900. Before then, fortunately, some were sent to European zoos and were used to build up a thriving herd at Woburn Abbey, the home of the Duke of Bedford. In 1986, thirty-nine descendants of these deer were returned to China for eventual release into reserves specially created for them.

Other species, not yet extinct in the wild but in imminent danger of becoming so, have had their dwindling populations helped by the introduction of specimens bred in captivity. On the Hawaiian islands, many native species of birds were wiped

The wild nene population has now risen to about 2,000. At one time, there were only a handful of these birds on Hawaii.

out after the islands were overrun by dogs and cats introduced by foreigners. One species that has survived is the Hawaiian goose, or nene, but it owes its continued existence at least in part to the reintroduction of birds bred at Sir Peter Scott's Wildfowl Trust centers in England. Mauritius, once home of the dodo, has lost many other species too. Some that remain, such as the pink pigeon, are seriously threatened and are the subject of captive breeding projects both on Mauritius and at the Jersey Zoo in the Channel Islands, with the ultimate aim of releasing them back into the wild.

Reintroduction projects are still in their infancy and they still present a number of problems. One is that it is futile to reintroduce animals if there are only insufficient or unsuitable habitats available for them. Clearly, conserving the habitat is at least as important as conserving the individual species that live in it. For a number of reasons, animals that are the product of several generations of captive breeding may be less able to survive in the wild.

A radio collar is put on this tiger so that it can be tracked over long distances. Information about an animal's behavior is vital if it is to be protected effectively.

The most important factor in the reestablishment of an animal in its original range is the presence of a suitable habitat. Many areas have been drastically altered since the time when their natural fauna was still abundant, and many animal species may not be sufficiently adaptable to reestablish themselves in such modified environments.

For example, they may have been "softened" by captive life, they may have become used to different diets and may be genetically less suited to such an existence than their wild counterparts. Release projects try to take these factors into account by affording the subjects for release a measure of protection before they are actually set free. This usually involves keeping them confined in their new surroundings for some time, while they adapt to various changes, such as the climate and the available food. Once liberated, their movements and behavior need to be carefully studied in order to find out how successfully they are adapting to their new life.

With certain species, it is possible to increase breeding success by careful control of wild populations, particularly of egg-laying species such as birds and reptiles. Many reptiles, such as crocodiles, tortoises, turtles and lizards, produce large numbers of young of which relatively few survive to maturity due to natural predation by other species. If the eggs of rare species are collected and hatched under controlled conditions, predation can be avoided and much greater numbers of young can be reared to the stage where they are relatively safe from attack before being released into the wild. At the Charles Darwin Research Station on the Galapagos Islands, eggs from some

of the rarest surviving kinds of tortoises are hatched artificially and the young reared for several years before being set free. This allows them to grow sufficiently large to avoid being killed by the introduced predators, such as dogs and pigs. On some of the islands these animals have eaten all the young tortoises under a certain size, so that artificial hatching has proved the only way of adding young animals to the population. Similar projects have been undertaken with other endangered reptiles, such as marine turtles and some species of crocodile, like the fish-eating gharial of India and Nepal.

For some animals, preparation for a life in the wild requires considerable training. Until recently, large numbers of young orangutans were captured each year in Borneo and Sumatra, a process that

Marine turtles leave their eggs buried on open beaches as the young are very vulnerable to predators when they hatch out.

involved killing their mothers to obtain the infants, which were then kept as pets or sold to animal dealers. Now the Indonesian government has banned this cruel practice, and any young orangutans found in illegal captivity are sent to special rehabilitation centers in the forests, where they are taught to lead a natural existence once again. This is a time-consuming and expensive business but, with only a few thousand orangutans living in the wild, every one successfully returned to the forests in this way represents a valuable contribution to the survival of the species.

Sometimes, the only way to save a species from extinction is to risk losing it altogether. In 1941, there were less than fifteen whooping cranes known to exist in North America. The plan to save them involved removing some of the eggs from the last few pairs and fostering them under a more common species, the sandhill

Whooping cranes were endangered by the drainage of the Texan marshes where they spent the winter months.

crane. Biologists had observed that, although the whooping cranes laid two eggs in a clutch, they rarely raised two chicks. So the project was aimed at increasing the reproductive success of the birds. Fortunately, the gamble paid off and today whooping crane populations are steadily increasing again, with the help of carefully managed captive breeding and fostering programs.

The whooping crane story demonstrates the value of scientific knowledge in the fight to save endangered species. For a lot of other species with dangerously low population levels, our knowledge of their behavior is woefully limited – a major disadvantage in any effort to save them from extinction.

37

6
The future

"'Tis not too late to seek a newer world."
Alfred Lord Tennyson

"And God spake, saying 'Bring forth
every living thing, of all flesh, both of
fowl and of cattle and of every
creeping thing that creepeth upon the
earth, that they may breed
abundantly and be fruitful and
multiply upon the earth.'"
Genesis: Chapter Eight

It is estimated that there are between five
and ten million species of living organisms
sharing this planet with us. So far we have
been considering some of the more
noteworthy species among the mammals,
birds and reptiles. But what about the
other end of the scale of life? Compara-
tively little is known about the status of
fish, invertebrates or plants, of which
millions of forms abound. How many of
them are endangered? By identifying the
problems surrounding the larger creatures that are threatened, we have only
really made a start. The plight of a
rhinoceros may not seem comparable
with that of a spider, a leech or a crab,
yet every life form should be of equal
importance. Only now are we beginning
to identify some of the species most at risk
among these forms of life. Who would have
thought, for example, that a species of
leech could become extinct? But the
medicinal leech, which was widely used

in the nineteenth century for bloodletting,
is now vanishing from many of its European haunts. This is the result of heavy
overcollecting in the past, combined with
the loss of many of the ponds and marsh-
lands in which it formerly lived. Recently,
there has been fresh demand for this
species, which is used in research work
on human blood clotting. Efforts are therefore being made both to protect the surviving colonies of leeches and also to raise
them under laboratory conditions.

The medicinal leech has long been
known to us because it has been of value,
but how many other species are in danger
of becoming extinct, even before they
become known to science? Cataloging all
the earth's living organisms is an almost
impossible task, so how are we going to
know which of them are in the greatest
need of help? One solution to this problem

*A large copper butterfly. Many species
of butterflies are in danger from habitat
loss, collectors and pesticides.*

is to try to provide "blanket" protection for as many wildlife habitats as possible. A prime example we have already considered is the tropical rain forest, long recognized as among the richest, most diverse and most important ecosystems on earth. Yet, despite this, their disappearance continues unabated. At the current rate of loss, many countries will have sacrificed all their remaining rain forests within the next twenty years. Since they contain almost half the animal and plant species known to science, such a loss would be immeasurable. Much the same applies to grasslands, wetlands, marine habitats, in fact all of the remaining wild places on earth.

For several years now, the WWF and other conservation bodies have been trying to remedy this problem by putting pressure on the governments of many

The wasteland that remains after rain forest has been destroyed.

countries to draw up conservation plans at both national and international levels. While the human population continues to soar, we cannot "put back the clock" for we will have an ever-increasing need to utilize more of the earth's remaining wild habitats. But if guidelines can be promoted and accepted as to how best to manage these areas, there is a far better outlook for the wildlife they contain. This is the aim of the World Conservation Strategy, which was launched in 1980 in response to the actions of certain countries that have particularly poor records in conservation. Its aim is to coordinate governmental controls of land usage (especially habitat destruction) and various other factors affecting wildlife with recom-

mendations from conservation groups on how to improve matters. As a result of the initial effort, a number of countries around the world are now preparing their own national conservation strategies.

There is a growing awareness that the protection of the environment as a whole, rather than the protection of individual species, is the real key to the problem. In the meantime, we are facing the unenviable task of trying to decide, with the limited funds and manpower available, which species are in the most urgent need of protection. Often, it is an impossibly difficult decision to make.

In North America, desperate efforts are being made to save the threatened Californian condor, now reduced to a handful of specimens in the wild. Vast amounts of money and time have been spent on trying to preserve this magnificent bird. The latest project involved capturing most of the survivors for a captive breeding and reintroduction program. The attempt has been strongly criticized on the grounds that such an enormous outlay is unjustified on a species that might very soon become extinct anyway, despite all the attempts to save it. Would it not be better to concentrate such expenditure on, say, creating or improving reserves that help the chances of survival for a whole range of species? There is no doubt that single species protection programs often do work, but seen against the much greater problems facing us today they have begun to represent an outmoded approach to conservation.

Left The future of the Californian condor is still far from assured, despite all the money that has been spent on its protection.

Conservation or Preservation?
Conservation embraces the positive and dynamic science of ecology, the study of living processes and their interdependence on each other and their habitat. Preservation on the other hand is concerned with the strictest protection of an individual species. In some cases, it is the only way of saving the remaining populations of endangered animals.

Today, the accent is on the protection of habitats, not merely for the benefit of the individual endangered species that they contain, but in their entirety. This approach has many advantages. The animals and plants that make up natural ecosystems represent one of the greatest natural resources available to humankind. Carefully managed, these resources may be tapped without detriment to them and to our benefit. There is an increasing trend toward the idea that wildlife conservation must pay in some way. In Africa, for example, wild game animals use their habitat far more efficiently than do domestic species such as cattle. In a number of African countries, "wildlife farming" is increasingly being seen as a way of providing people with a more economic source of meat. Then there is the revenue that can be gained from tourism. If wildlife reserves and parks are seen to be profitable, there is a greater incentive for their creation and maintenance. The principle behind the World Conservation Strategy is that we should not destroy that which is useful to us, or might be found to be useful to us in future. But if this is the only basis on which wildlife conservation is seen to be acceptable, many creatures that have apparently little or unknown economic value are put at a disadvantage in the long list of species waiting to be conserved. And if we should find alternative answers to our needs, then these economics of conservation would quickly become questionable.

Perhaps the most important task is to educate the peoples of the world about the need for effective conservation of wildlife and natural resources, whether for economic, social or aesthetic reasons. There is an innate desire in many people, not only in the West but all over the world, to have access to wild and open natural landscapes, or at least to know that they are "there." This is a powerful weapon in the conservationist's armory.

Yet the problems of achieving success still remain. Set against some of the other major issues facing the world today (such as the famine in Africa, the continued threat of nuclear war and the arms race), concern over what is happening to the world's wildlife may seem relatively unimportant. But the extinction of a species goes far beyond merely the irredeemable loss of yet another form of life. It encompasses the much broader issues of our view of ourselves and our own importance, our role in the world and the effect we are having on it. Have we the right to "play God" and decide which species shall survive and which shall die? Or do we have a duty to protect and preserve the delicate balance of flora and fauna on earth – a duty we ignore at our own peril?

Right *These beautiful orchids have evolved to look like bees. Our incentive to save them must be aesthetic, as they have no known economic value.*

Below *Wildlife safaris for tourists are a major source of income in East Africa.*

Glossary

Aesthetic   Relating to beauty.

Alien species   Animals and plants that are introduced to an area where they were unknown before.

Conservation   The protection, preservation and careful management of natural resources and the environment.

Deforestation   The clearance of trees on a massive scale.

Developed World   The rich industrialized countries of North America, Europe, Australia and New Zealand, and the Eastern bloc.

Ecology   The study of the relationships between living organisms and their environment.

Ecosystem   A system involving the interactions between a community and its environment.

Evolution   A gradual change in the characteristics of a population over successive generations.

Fauna   All the animal life of a given place.

Flora   All the plant life of a given place.

Food chain   A series of organisms in a community. Each one feeds on organisms lower down the food chain and is itself eaten by organisms higher up the chain.

Habitat   The natural home of species.

Herbivore   An animal that feeds on grass and other plants.

Indigenous   Originating or occuring naturally in a country or region.

Marsupial   A mammal whose young are born in an immature state and continue development in the mother's *marsupium*, or pouch, e.g. the kangaroo.

Musk   A strong-smelling glandular secretion of the male musk deer that is used in perfumes.

Poaching   Catching animals, usually game or fish, illegally.

Predation   A relationship between two species of animal in a community, in which one (the predator) hunts, kills and eats the other (the prey).

Primate   Any placental mammal of the order *Primates*, typically having flexible hands and feet with opposable first digits, good eyesight and, in the higher apes, a highly developed brain.

Rain forests   Dense forest found in tropical areas of heavy rainfall.

Rehabilitation   Helping someone or something readapt to a certain set of circumstances.

Reintroduction   Returning a species that has become extinct in the wild to its natural environment, having rescued a few specimens before the final extinction and reared them in special zoos or reserves.

Reptile   A cold-blooded vertebrate, usually with an outer covering of horny scales or plates, e.g. tortoises, snakes, crocodiles

Soil erosion   The loss of the fertile topsoil (made up of disintegrated rock particles, humus, water and air) due to overfarming, deforestation or poor agricultural methods.

Specimen   An individual regarded as typical of a group or class to which it belongs.

Steppes   An extensive grassy plain, usually without trees.

Toxic   Poisonous.

Utilize   To make practical or worthwhile use of.

Index

Africa 23, 41–2
Arabian oryx 28, 32

Beaver 21
Blaawbok 14
Buffalo 10
Butterflies 38

Californian condor 40–1
Captive breeding programs 28, 32–7, 41
Chimpanzee 18
China 25–6, 34
Conservation 18–19, 23, 42
Convention on International Trade in Endangered Species (CITES) 30–1

Dinosaurs 9
Dodo 13–14
Domestic animals 12, 13
Dusky seaside sparrow 15

Economic importance of wildlife 8, 22, 41–2
Education 29, 42
Elephants 19, 23
European bison 21, 33
Extinct species 9, 14
Extinction 8, 9–15, 16, 38–41

Fauna and Flora Preservation Society (FFPS) 28
Fostering programs 37
Fur trade 29

Galapagos Islands 12, 36
Gibbon 18
Gorillas 18
   Mountain Gorilla Project 29
Great Auk 14

Habitat
   conservation 19, 35, 39
   destruction 12, 15, 17–18, 22, 25–6, 29, 39
Hawaii, 12, 34–5
Huia 15
Hunting 10, 23
   overhunting 10, 27–8

India 25
International Council for Bird Preservation (ICBP) 24
International Union for Conservation of Nature and Natural Resources (IUCN) 24, 39
International Whaling Commission (INC) 27–8
Invertebrates 38
Ivory 19

Leech, medicinal 38
Lemurs 18

Madagascar 18
Mauritius 13

National Parks 21, 23, 41
Nene 34–5
New Zealand 12
North America 21, 41

Oceans 20
   pollution of 20–1
Orangutan 18, 36–7
Overgrazing 12

Pandas 25–6
Passenger pigeon 10
Pere David's deer 33–4
Poaching 19, 23, 29

Polar regions 19–20
Przewalski's Horse 33

Quagga 14

Rain forests 18
   destruction 17, 39
Red Data Books 24
Reintroduction programs 28, 32–7
Reptiles 30
Rhinoceros 19, 24

Saber-toothed tiger 9
Science, role in conservation 26, 35–7
Solitaire 13
South America 18, 19
Steller's sea cow 15

Tarantula, red-kneed 31
Tasmanian wolf 15

Tiger
   Project Tiger 25
Tourism 29, 41–2
Trade in animals and animal products 29–31
Turtle 36

Whaling 20, 27–8
Whooping crane 37
Wildfowl Trust 35
Wildlife farming 41
Wildlife reserves 21, 41
Woolly mammoth 10
World Conservation Strategy 39–41
World Wildlife Fund 24, 39

Zoos 32–3

© Copyright 1987 Wayland (Publishers) Ltd
61 Western Road, Hove, East Sussex
BN3 1JD, England